Deadly Dinos

By K. C. Kelley

The Child's World®
www.childsworld.com

Published in the United States of America by The Child's World®
P.O. Box 326 • Chanhassen, MN 55317-0326
800-599-READ • www.childsworld.com

ACKNOWLEDGMENTS

The Child's World®: Mary Berendes, Publishing Director

Produced by Shoreline Publishing Group LLC
President / Editorial Director: James Buckley, Jr.
Designer: Tom Carling, carlingdesign.com
Cover Art: Slimfilms
Copy Editor: Beth Adelman

Photo Credits
Cover—Slimfilms
Interior—Davide Bonnadonna: 19; Corbis: 5, 11, 18, 27;
Dreamstime.com: 17, 27; Getty Images: 13, 15, 23, 24; iStock: 10,
25; Todd Marshall: 9, 21, 28; Science Source: 6, 12

LIBRARY OF CONGRESS CATALOGING-IN-PUBLICATION DATA

Kelley, K. C.
  Deadly dinos / by K.C. Kelley.
     p. cm. — (Boys rock!)
  Includes bibliographical references and index.
  ISBN 1-59296-728-0 (lib. bdg. : alk. paper)
  1. Dinosaurs—Juvenile literature. 2. Carnivora, Fossil—Juvenile
literature. I. Title. II. Series.
  QE861.5.K45 2006
  567.912—dc22

                          2006009021

CONTENTS

SMALL BUT Deadly

To see monkeys, tigers, or penguins, you can always go to a zoo or watch television. But where can you go to see real dinosaurs? Nowhere! You'd need to travel back in time for millions and millions of years. In fact, you'd need to travel back to a time period called the *Mesozoic Era*, between 248 and 65 million years ago. The world was a very different place back then!

How different? For one thing, the huge land areas we call **continents** weren't where they are now. In fact, at the beginning of the Mesozoic, they were all pushed together into a giant continent called *Pangaea* (pan-JEE-uh). The weather was milder, too, and the oceans were higher. There were lots of different kinds of dinosaurs. How do we know? Because we find their **fossils**—their remains turned to stone.

Here someone carefully cleans off a fossilized Eoraptor skull some 228 million years old.

This Brachiosaurus lived about 175 million years ago and was 80 feet (24 m) long. Even huge plant-eaters like this weren't completely safe from predators.

Scientists looking at dinosaur fossil teeth can tell that some dinosaurs were **herbivores**, or plant-eaters. Others were **carnivores**, or meat-eaters. Many of the carnivores got their meat by hunting and killing other dinosaurs. Meat-eating dinosaurs had sharp teeth and claws and walked on their two back legs. Their front legs were usually smaller—perfect for slashing and holding things.

When Did They Live?

Scientists divide the Mesozoic Era into three smaller time periods:

Triassic (248 to 208 million years ago)—the first dinosaurs and **mammals**.

Jurassic (208 to 144 million years ago)—lots of dinosaurs and the first birds.

Cretaceous (creh-TAY-shuss) (145 to 65 million years ago)—even more dinosaurs.

At the end of the Cretaceous Period, many kinds of animals died out—including all the dinosaurs. Why? Many people think a **comet** or **asteroid** hit the earth, kicking up dust that blocked sunlight and caused widespread changes.

Eoraptor (EE-oh-RAP-tor) is the earliest meat-eating dinosaur ever discovered—in fact, it's one of the earliest dinosaurs of all! It was small and lightly built, but its jaws held dozens of sharp teeth, perfect for tearing meat. It could walk upright and run fairly quickly on its two back legs.

Coelophysis (SEE-low-FY-sis) was another very early predator. It's much better known because of hundreds of *Coelophysis* skeletons found in New Mexico.

Slender and fast, this predator probably lived in groups. Remains found in the animal's stomach area show that *Coelophysis* ate fish and small reptiles—and other *Coelophysis*, too!

Standing 4 feet (1 m) tall, Coelophysis was also about 9 feet (3 m) long. It lived about 220 million years ago.

Tiny *Compsognathus* (KOMP-sog-NAY-thus) lived about 60 million years later than *Coelophysis*. Only two fossil *Compsognathus* have been found. This birdlike dinosaur probably ran very quickly on its back legs, using its long tail for balance. Its head was small and pointed, and its jaws held lots of sharp little teeth. What did it eat? Lizards and bugs, and maybe some small mammals.

Deinonychus slashed at prey with its claws and tore off chunks of flesh with its curved teeth.

Deinonychus (dye-NON-ih-kus) means "terrible claw." One good look will show you how this killing machine got its name! The second toe of each back foot had a wickedly sharp, curved claw about 5 inches (13 cm) long. *Deinonychus* had a fairly large brain and good eyesight—all the better to track down its **prey** in the dense brush.

This model shows what Deinonychus might have looked like when attacking.

Deinonychus was built for killing—and for speed. With its body held flat and its tail held stiff, it ran to attack on long, strong legs. At one fossil bed, several *Deinonychus* were found together, so scientists think they might have hunted in packs. *Velociraptor* (veh-LOSS-ih-RAP-tor) was smaller than

Five against one? That's not fair! Maybe not, but this is how Deinonychus might have hunted.

an adult human and lived in what is now Asia. It looked somewhat like *Deinonychus*, but it wasn't as big. Like *Deinonychus*, *Velociraptor* might have hunted in packs. This predator was smart and fast (but not as supersmart or superfast as it appeared in the movie *Jurassic Park*).

Velociraptor was only about 3 feet (1 m) tall and 6 feet (2 m) long. It lived about 85 million years ago.

A Handy Toe

Velociraptor had a large claw on its middle toe. Recent studies suggest that it might have used the claw for clinging to an animal rather than slashing it open.

The 8-foot (2-m) long Protoceratops was a plant-eater with a large, fan-shaped bony plate around the top of its head.

One of the most exciting fossil finds of all time was in the desert of Mongolia, near China. The fossils showed a *Velociraptor* and a plant-eating *Protoceratops* in a fight to the death. The *Velociraptor's* claw is stuck in the neck of the *Protoceratops*, and the *Protoceratops* seems to have bitten and broken the *Velociraptor's* arm.

Troodon (TROH-uh-don) was roughly the same size as *Velociraptor*. It probably lived in cooler regions. Its brain size suggests that it was very smart, and its large eyes would have helped it hunt in poor light—perhaps at dawn or dusk.

Slender and quick, Troodon *used its long tail for balance.* Troodon *stood about 3 feet (1 m) tall and was about 8 feet (2 m) long.*

BIGGER
Eaters

Some of those meat-eating dinosaurs were pretty scary, but there were some much bigger, scarier ones! *Allosaurus* lived at about the same time as the chicken-sized *Compsognathus*, but it was much, much larger. There were lots of *Allosaurus*, too. In the Late Jurassic Period, they were the largest, most common meat-eating dinosaurs in the area we call western North America.

These powerful predators walked on two sturdy back legs and could run as fast as 20 miles (32 km) per hour. Their short arms ended in three-fingered hands that had claws up

Allosaurus *had teeth that were 2 to 4 inches (5 to 10 cm) long, and bony bumps on its head. This predator stood about 17 feet (5 m) tall and was 40 feet (12 m) long.*

to 6 inches (15 cm) long. They had very sharp teeth, too. *Allosaurus* probably hunted large plant-eating dinosaurs.

Compare this human hand to the claw of Baryonyx. *Big, huh?* Baryonyx stood 6 feet (2 m) tall and was about 30 feet (9 m) long.

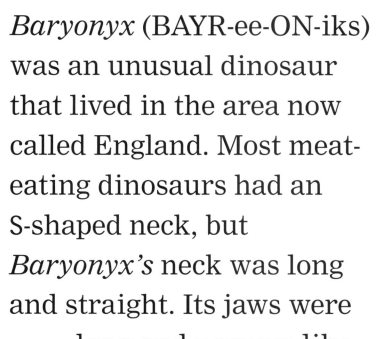

Baryonyx (BAYR-ee-ON-iks) was an unusual dinosaur that lived in the area now called England. Most meat-eating dinosaurs had an S-shaped neck, but *Baryonyx's* neck was long and straight. Its jaws were long and narrow, like those of a crocodile, and it had more than 100 teeth! Its front legs were shorter than its back legs. On each hand, *Baryonyx* had an amazing oversized claw more than 12 inches (30 cm) long! *Baryonyx* probably ate lots

of fish. One skeleton had the fossilized remains of the animal's last meal in its stomach area—fish scales, as well as bones from fish and a young plant-eating dinosaur called an *Iguanadon*.

Baryonyx had teeth like those of some modern fish-eating animals. It might have eaten other animals as well as fish.

The scary-looking *Spinosaurus* (SPY-no-SAWR-us) lived in what is now Africa. It was huge! Its most amazing feature was a large "sail" held up by bony spines 6 feet (2 m) high. Unusual backbones let the dinosaur arch its back, perhaps to spread its sail like a fan or a peacock's tail.

What was the "sail" used for? Nobody knows for sure. It might have helped balance the dinosaur's body temperature by soaking up warmth in the sunshine.

Because of the shape of its teeth, *Spinosaurus* has often been pictured as a fish-eater. It might have eaten other dinosaurs and animals too, including flying ones!

Spinosaurus *most likely lived near the water, making one of its favorite meals (fish) easy to find.*

TYRANNOSAURUS Rex

And now—on to the most famous of all the dinosaurs. From the enormous head to its claw-tipped toes, it's the kind of creature you see in nightmares—and in scary movies!

What is this meat-eating monster? It's the mighty and dangerous *Tyrannosaurus rex*, or *T. rex* for short.

Tyrannosaurus lived near the end of the age of dinosaurs. There were actually several different kinds of *Tyrannosaurus*, but *T. rex* is the best known.

T. Rex *lived about 67 million years ago. It stood 18 feet (5 m) tall and was as much as 41 feet (12 m) long.*

Here's Sue at the Field Museum in Chicago. Sue's skull is 5 feet (2 m) long and weighs 600 pounds (272 kg)!

Scientists know more about *T. rex* than they do about any other meat-eating dinosaur. Why? Because so many *T. rex* fossils have been found in Mongolia and western North America.

The most complete, famous *T. rex* skeleton has been nicknamed "Sue." Nobody's really sure if Sue was a girl or a boy, because that can be hard to tell from just bones. The bones do show that Sue was 29 years old—very old for a *Tyrannosaurus*.

Doesn't this T. rex foot look like the foot of a bird? Scientists think dinosaurs and today's birds are very closely related.

Years ago, people thought *T. rex* was slow and plodding. Not true! *T. rex* walked upright, with its tail held out behind it for balance. It could run, too.

T. rex's hind legs were big and sturdy. Its arms were short—only 3 feet (1 m) long—but they were very strong. At the ends of its arms, *T. rex* had hands with two fingers. Its head held big, extremely powerful jaws with 50 to 60 cone-shaped, bone-crunching teeth. If one

Lots to Learn

Scientists are busy studying *T. rex* fossils to learn all they can. For example, were *T. rex* just hunters, or were they also **scavengers** that ate dead animals? (Best guess? They were probably both.) Also, did you know that a *T. rex* grew fastest during its teenage years (13 to 17)? That's when it put on an amazing 5 pounds (2 kg) a day!

tooth fell out, another grew in to replace it! Was *T. rex* the biggest of all the meat-eating dinosaurs? Probably not—there were other big predators, too.

These statues show T. rex *attacking a plant-eating* Triceratops.

Giganotosaurus (jih-GAN-oh-toh-SAWR-us), found in what is now South America, isn't as well known as *T. rex,* but it might have been slightly larger. Other dinosaurs discovered in Argentina and Morocco are huge, too.

Giganotosaurus *lived about 95 million years ago. It was 49 feet (15 m) longer than a* T. rex*!*

It's too bad we can't really travel back in time! If we could, we could watch real dinosaurs in action. We could see how they moved, what they ate, and how they raised their young.

In the meantime, scientists keep learning more by uncovering and studying more dinosaur fossils. From a nestful of dinosaur eggs to a patch of fossilized skin, each discovery provides exciting information. There will be new finds every year—so stay tuned!

GLOSSARY

asteroid a rocky object, smaller than a planet, that travels around the Sun

carnivores animals that eat only meat

comet a frozen mass of ice, dust, gases, and rock pieces that travels around the Sun

continents huge land masses that are largely surrounded by water

fossils the remains of ancient animals or plants that have slowly turned to stone

herbivores animals that eat only plants

mammals animals that have warm bodies and feed their babies milk from their bodies

predators animals that hunt, kill, and eat other animals

prey animals that are killed and eaten by other animals

reptiles animals that have backbones, lungs, and tough skin covered with scales, and that need outside heat to warm their bodies

scavengers animals that eat the bodies of dead animals they happen to find

FIND OUT MORE

BOOKS

The Complete Guide to Prehistoric Life
by Tim Haines and Paul Chambers
(Firefly Books, Richmond Hill, Ontario, Canada) 2006
Describes more than a hundred of Earth's early creatures,
including what they looked like and how they lived.

Dino Wars: The Dinosaurs' Biggest, Baddest Battles
by Jinny Johnson and Michael Benton
(Abrams Books for Young Readers, New York) 2005
A lively look at the fighting side of dinosaurs, including what
battles between different kinds of dinosaurs might have been
like.

Eyewitness Dinosaur
by David Norman and Angela Milner
(DK Publishing, New York) 2004
This book features dozens of pictures of different dinosaurs.

Meat-Eating Dinosaurs
by Thom Holmes and Laurie Holmes
(Enslow Publishers, Berkeley Heights, NJ) 2001
Everything you want to know about dinosaur-eating dinosaurs.

WEB SITES

Visit our home page for lots of links about dinosaurs and their
world: www.childsworld.com/links

Note to Parents, Teachers, and Librarians: We routinely check our Web links to
make sure they're safe, active sites—so encourage your readers to check them out!

INDEX

California-based author **K. C. KELLEY** has written many books for young readers on topics such as baseball, football, motor sports, soccer, dolphins, rockets, and history.